Donna Kooler's 555 Country Cross-Stitch Patterns

Donna Kooler's 555 Country Cross-Stitch Patterns

Sterling Publishing Co., Inc. New York
A Sterling/Chapelle Book

Kooler Design Studio, Inc.

Editor: Priscilla Timm
President: Donna Kooler
Executive Vice President: Linda Gillum
Vice President: Priscilla Timm
Creative Director: Deanna West
Executive Assistant: Loretta Heden
Design Staff: Linda Gillum, Nancy Rossi,
Barbara Baatz, Jorja Hernandez, and Sandy Orton
Contributing Artists: Donna Yuen and Pam Johnson
Staff: Sara Angle, Anita Forfang, Virginia Hanley-Rivett,
Marsha Hinkson, Arlis Johnson, Lori Patton,
Char Randolph, and Giana Shaw

Dedication

Our, studio was filled with an extra bit of laughter, chatter, and friendship while working upon this challenging project. It might be equated to a bee. Everyone was eagerly contributing something of value, their artistic talents, wonderful creative ideas, and beautiful stitching. The results of all this talent is a wonderful patchwork collection of over 500 cross-stitch designs bound together for your creative enjoyment.

We wanted the chapters to express our feeling for home and family as well as the giving and sharing that cross-stitchers always exhibit. So, we would like to dedicate this book to all who share this love and pass along personal expressions of beauty while creating future heirlooms for generations to come.

Library of Congress Cataloging-in-Publication Data

Kooler, Donna.
    [555 county cross-stitch patterns]
    Donna Kooler's 555 country cross-stitch patterns.
        p.   cm.
    "A Sterling/Chapelle book."
    Includes index.
    ISBN 0-8069-0330-9
    1. Cross-stitch—Patterns. 2. Decoration and ornament, Rustic.
    I. Title.
    TT778.C76K64 1998   97-44762
        746.44'3041—dc21   CIP
10 9 8 7 6 5 4 3 2

Published by Sterling Publishing Company, Inc.,
387 Park Avenue South, New York, NY 10016
© 1998 by Chapelle Limited
Distributed in Canada by Sterling Publishing
℅ Canadian Manda Group, One Atlantic Avenue, Suite 105, Toronto, Ontario,
Canada M6K 3E7
Distributed in Great Britain and Europe by Cassell PLC, Wellington House, 125
Strand, London WC2R 0BB, England
Distributed in Australia by Capricorn Link (Australia) Pty Ltd., P.O. Box 6651,
Baulkham Hills, Business Centre, NSW 2153, Australia
Printed and Bound in United States
All rights reserved

Sterling ISBN 0-8069-0330-9

Chapelle Ltd.

Owner: Jo Packham
Editor: Karmen Quinney
Staff: Marie Barber, Ann Bear, Areta Bingham,
Kass Burchett, Rebecca Christensen, Marilyn Goff,
Amber Hansen, Shirley Heslop, Holly Hollingsworth,
Shawn Hsu, Susan Jorgensen, Pauline Locke,
Ginger Mikkelsen, Barbara Milburn, Linda Orton,
Rhonda Rainey, Leslie Ridenour, and Cindy Stoeckl
Photographer: Kevin Dilley Hazen Photography Studio
Photography Stylist: Leslie Liechty

If you have any questions or comments or would like information on specialty products featured in this book, please contact: Chapelle Ltd., Inc.,
P.O. Box 9252 Ogden, UT 84409
(801) 621-2777 • FAX (801) 621-2788

Contents

General Instructions

Introduction

Contained in this book are over 555 counted cross-stitch designs.

For each of the six chapters herein, samplers have been stitched and photographed. The samplers have been graphed and fall on the pages following the photograph.

The remaining designs in each chapter are not stitched nor photographed. Each page of graphed designs has its own color code.

To create one-of-a-kind motifs, vary colors in the graphed designs. The stitching possibilities will prove endless.

Fabric for Cross-stitch

Counted cross-stitch is usually worked on even-weave fabrics. These fabrics are manufactured specifically for counted-thread embroidery and are woven with the same number of vertical as horizontal threads per inch.

Because the number of threads in the fabric is equal in each direction, each stitch will be the same size. The number of threads per inch in even-weave fabrics determines the size of a finished design.

Number of Strands

The number of strands used per stitch varies depending on the fabric used. Generally, the rule to follow for cross-stitching is three strands on Aida 11, two strands on Aida 14, one or two strands on Aida 18 (depending on desired thickness of stitches) and one strand on Hardanger 22.

For back-stitching, use one strand on all fabrics. When completing a french knot, use two strands and one wrap on all fabrics.

Preparing Fabric

Cut fabric at least 3" larger on all sides than finished design size to ensure enough space for desired assembly. If the design is used to embellish a project that will be finished further, check instructions for specific fabric allowances. A 3" margin is the minimum amount of space that allows for comfortably finishing the edges of the design.

To prevent fraying, whipstitch or machine-zigzag along raw edges or apply liquid fray preventer.

Needles for Cross-stitch

Needles should slip easily through fabric holes without piercing fabric threads. For fabric with 11 or fewer threads per inch, use a tapestry needle size 24; for 14 threads per inch, use a tapestry needle size 24 or 26; for 18 or more threads per inch, use a tapestry needle size 26. Never leave needle in design area of fabric. It may leave rust or a permanent impression on fabric.

Finished Design Size

To determine size of finished design, divide stitch count by number of threads per inch of fabric. When design is stitched over two threads, divide stitch count by half the threads per inch.

Floss

For each sampler and each page of graphed designs there is a color code. All numbers and color names on this code represent DMC brands of floss. Use 18" lengths of floss. For best coverage, separate strands. Dampen with wet sponge. Then put together number of strands required for fabric used.

Centering the Design

Fold the fabric in half horizontally, then vertically. Place a pin in the fold point to mark the center. Locate the center of the design on the graph. To help in centering the samplers, arrows are provided at left center and top center. Begin stitching all designs at the center point of graph and fabric.

Securing the Floss

Insert needle up from the underside of the fabric at starting point. Hold 1" of thread behind the fabric and stitch over it, securing with the first few stitches. To finish thread, run under four or more stitches on the back of the design. Never knot floss, unless working on clothing.

Another method of securing floss is the waste knot. Knot floss and insert needle from the right side of the fabric about 1" from design area. Work several stitches over the thread to secure. Cut off the knot later.

Carrying Floss

To carry floss, weave floss under the previously worked stitches on the back. Do not carry thread across any fabric that is not or will not be stitched. Loose threads, especially dark ones, will show through the fabric.

Cleaning Completed Work

When stitching is complete, soak fabric in cold water with a mild soap for five to 10 minutes. Rinse well and roll in a towel to remove excess water. Do not wring. Place work face down on a dry towel and iron on warm setting until the fabric is dry.

Cross-stitch (X st)

Stitches are done in a row or, if necessary, one at a time in an area. Stitching is done by coming up through a hole between woven threads at A. Then, go down at B, the hole diagonally across from A. Come back up at C and down at D, etc. Complete the top stitches to create an "X". All top stitches should lie in the same direction. Come up at E and go down at B, come up at C and go down at F, etc.

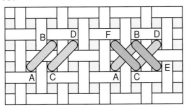

Backstitch (BS)

Pull the needle through at the point marked A. Then go down one opening to the right, at B. Then, come back up at C. Now, go down one opening to the right, this time at "A".

French Knot (FK)

Bring needle up at A, using two strands of embroidery floss. Loosely wrap floss once around needle. Place needle at B, next to A. Pull floss taut as needle is pushed down through fabric. Carry floss across back of work between knots.

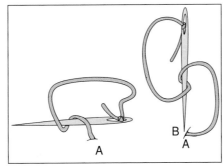

Long Stitch (LS)

Bring needle up at A; go down at B. Pull flat. Repeat A–B for each stitch. The length of the stitch should be the same as the length of the line on the design chart.

Lazy Daisy (LD)

Bring the needle up at A. Keep the thread flat, untwisted, and full. Put the needle down through fabric at B and up through at C, keeping the thread under the needle to form a loop. Pull the thread through, leaving the loop loose and full. To hold the loop in place, go down on other side of thread near C, forming a straight stitch over loop.

Bead Attachment (Bds)

Beads should sit facing the same direction as the top cross-stitch. Make first half of stitch in opposite direction from remainder of the piece. Come up as if to cross and pick up bead before going down in opposite corner. To strengthen stitch, come up again in lower corner and either go through bead again or split threads to lay around bead and go down in opposite corner.

Celebrations

Bottom Left

12

Bottom Middle

13

Bottom Right

DMC Floss				
	X st	**BS**	**FK**	**LS**
White	⊡			
3823	☐			
3078	◪			
745	△			
744	☐			
743	H			
742	✳			
725	⊡			
783		⌐		/
951	☐			
945	–			
3824	☐			
352	◎			
350	◼	⌐	●	
818	☐			
963	⊞			
3326	◻			/
961	◼	⌐	●	
223	◼			
3722		⌐		
3609	★			/
211	☐			
210	◻			
341	W			
747	☐			
3761	K			
807		⌐		
3756	⊠			
800	◻			
799	◼			
798	◼	⌐	●	
955	☐			
954	▨			
562		⌐		
989	◼			
988		⌐		
437	N			
3776	◼			
758	☐			
356	◼			
632	◼	⌐		
762	◻			
318	◼			
317		⌐	●	
310	◼	⌐	●	

DMC Floss

	X st		X st	BS	FK
White	·	964			
745		954	◎		
776	◎	738			
3609		437	+		
3608		3779			
211		453			
209		452			
340		451			
747		317			
828	−	413			
800	★	3799			·

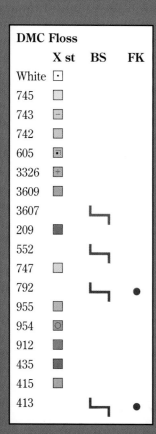

DMC Floss

	X st	BS	FK
White	⊡		
745	▢		
743	⊟		
742	▢		
605	⊡		
3326	⊞		
3609	▨		
3607		⌐	
209	▨		
552		⌐	
747	▢	⌐	
792		⌐	●
955	▨		
954	⊙		
912	▨		
435	▨		
415	▨		
413		⌐	●

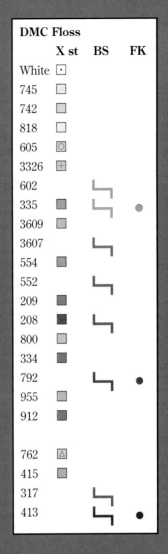

DMC Floss

	X st	BS	FK
White	·		
745			
742			
818			
605	○		
3326	+		
602		⌐	
335		⌐	●
3609			
3607		⌐	
554			
552		⌐	
209			
208		⌐	
800			
334			
792		⌐	●
955			
912			
762	△		
415			
317		⌐	
413		⌐	●

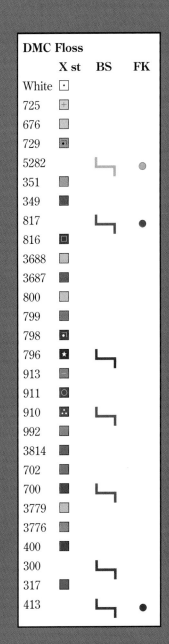

DMC Floss

	X st	BS	FK
White	·		
725	+		
676			
729	·		
5282		⌐	●
351			
349			
817		⌐	●
816	▣		
3688			
3687			
800			
799			
798	▪		
796	★	⌐	
913			
911	◉		
910	▦	⌐	
992			
3814			
702			
700		⌐	
3779			
3776			
400			
300		⌐	
317	■		
413		⌐	●

DMC Floss

	X st	BS	FK		X st	BS	FK
White	⊡			334	■		
744	☐			312	■	⌐	●
742	△			913	■		
725	+			912	◉		
676	▣			910	■		
729	■			702	■		
351	■			701	■	⌐	
350	■			699	■		
349	■			301	■		
817		⌐	●	415	☐		
775	☐	⌐		413	■	⌐	●

DMC Floss

	X st	BS	FK
White	⊡		
3822	▨		
3820	▨		
5282		⌐	
951	▨		
3340	▨		
3712	▨		
349	▨	⌐	
775	▨		
794	▨		
792		⌐	
702	▨	⌐	●
913	▨		
911	▨		
909	▨	⌐	
301	▨	⌐	
300	▨	⌐	
317	▨		
413	▨	⌐	●

DMC Floss

	X st	BS		X st	BS	FK
White	·		954	▨		
3823	▢		913	◉		
3822	▨		911	▩		
5282	▨	⌐	909		⌐	
951	▨		3776	▨		
351	▨		301	▨		
349	▩		400		⌐	
962	▨		317	▨		
775	▨		413	▩	⌐	●
322	▨	⌐				

DMC Floss

	X st	BS		X st	BS		X st	BS		X st	BS
White	·		3340	■		563	■		561		⌐
745	☐		963	☐		605	☐		702	■	⌐
744	☐		962	■		603		⌐	699		⌐
743	+		961	H		209	■		317		⌐
3045		⌐	3325	⊡		562	■		3799		⌐
3341	⊠										

DMC Floss

	X st	BS		X st	BS		X st	BS		X st	BS
White	·		957			552			907		
743			335			800			904		
741			326			334			413		
740			210			517					
946			208			472					

DMC Floss

	X st	BS		X st	BS		X st	BS
White			666			3811		
3689			211			959		
605			209			958		
894			3752			436		
3705								

Favorite Things

Lighthouses

A B C D

EFGH

IJKLMNO

Code for Pages 30-33

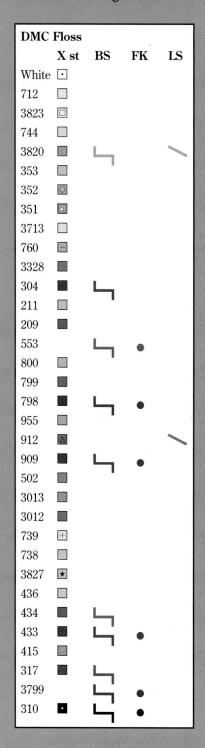

DMC Floss

	X st	BS	FK	LS
White	·			
712				
3823				
744				
3820	▨	⌐		/
353				
352	◎			
351				
3713				
760	−			
3328				
304	■	⌐		
211				
209				
553		⌐	●	
800				
799				
798	■	⌐	●	
955				
912	△			/
909	■	⌐	●	
502				
3013				
3012				
739	+			
738				
3827	★			
436				
434	■	⌐		
433	■	⌐	●	
415				
317	■	⌐		
3799		⌐	●	
310	■	⌐	●	

Code for Pages 34-35

DMC Floss

	X st	BS		X st	BS		X st	BS
White	·		961		⌐	597	■	
745			794	■		3809		⌐
744	−		3807		⌐	436		
743	◎		932	■		434		⌐
741		⌐	931	■		612	■	
352	■		930	■		610		⌐
350	■		955	■		762		
817	■	⌐	912	■		318	■	
963			367	■		317		⌐
3716	+		3815	■		310	■	⌐
962	■							

34

DMC Floss

	X st	BS		X st	BS		X st	BS	FK
White	·		946			437			
677			554	◎		435			
745	◎		552			434	+		
743	+		3607			898			●
742			800			762			
726			798	■		415	▣		
729			791			318			
351			912	⊡		317	★		
350			958			413			
349			739			3799	■		●

DMC Floss

	X st	BS		X st	BS	FK
White	·		702	■		
Ecru	–		3756	■		
745	△		3761	⊠		
744	■		563	N		
3827	+		562	■	⌐	
740	■		436	♥		
3341	○		739	■		
335	■		435	■		
211	■		433	■		
209	■		318	■	⌐	
3608	■		317		⌐	
3325	+	⌐	413	■	⌐	
334	■		310	▣		●
798	■	⌐				

DMC Floss

	X st	BS	FK
White	⊡		
745	▢		
744	−	⌐	
3827	⊞		
946	H		
3341		⌐	
899		⌐	
353	◎		
350	■	⌐	
666		⌐	
209	▨		
208		⌐	
800	⊠		
3755	▨		
3325	⊞		
826	■	⌐	
799	▧		
798		⌐	
796		⌐	
987		⌐	
955	▢		
912	✳		
921	■		
415	▨		
3799	■	⌐	●

DMC Floss

	X st	BS		X st	BS		X st	BS		X st	BS		X st	BS	FK
White	·		963	▨		211	▨		959	▬		436	♥		⌐
Ecru	−		776	⊠		210	▲		958	▪	⌐	920			⌐
712	▢		3326	H		209	▪		563	▪		838	▪		⌐
745	◎		353	◎		208	▪	⌐	702	▪		318	▪		
743	✳		335		⌐	775	▨		988	N		413	▪	⌐	•
742	⊡		666	▪		826	▪		986	▪	⌐	3799	▪	⌐	•
740	▪		3609	▨		322	▪	⌐	437	▢					
3341	△		3607	▪		798	▪								

39

DMC Floss

	X st	BS	FK
White	·		
744	+		
743			
972			
350	✻		
666		⌐	
946		⌐	
828	—		
798			
796	△		
435			
318			
413		⌐	
3799		⌐	●

DMC Floss								
X st		X st	FK		X st		X st	BS	FK
745		349			826		415		
743		666		●	931		318		
725		814			563		413		
776		209			702		3799		
899	M	775			437		310		●
351		3325	+		435				●

DMC Floss

	X st	BS
White	⊡	
746	◪	
745	▨	
744	⊟	⌐
740		⌐
3708	⊟	
3705	▨	
353	◎	
352	▨	
350		⌐
666	▨	⌐
498	⊡	⌐
211	▨	
209	▨	
208		⌐
775	▨	
3325	⊞	
798	■	⌐
369	▨	
368	◎	
367		⌐
987		⌐
504	▨	
3817	▽	
3815		⌐
739	▨	
738	⊞	
437	⊡	
436	⊠	
434		⌐
841	▨	⌐
801		⌐

DMC Floss

	X st	BS		X st	BS
White	⊡		823	◉	
746	⊿		739	▢	
352	▨		738	⊞	
666		⌐	436	⊠	
498		⌐	434		⌐
224	▨		842	▨	
223	▨		841	▨	⌐
3721		⌐	801		⌐
312	▪		762	▨	
336	■		414		⌐
939		⌐			

DMC Floss

	X st	BS		X st	BS		X st	BS	FK
White	·		335	▨		958	▨	⌐	
Ecru	—		326	▨	⌐	563	N	⌐	
745	▢		211	▨		562		⌐	
743	⊡		210	△		3774	▢		
3827	▨		209	▨		3779	▣		
783	▨	⌐	800	▨		3778	▨		
781	△		3325	⊞		632	▨	⌐	
3341	◯		334	▨		762	▢		
605	✳		798	▨		318	▨		
603	▨	⌐	312	▨	⌐	317	✳	⌐	
776	▨		964	▨		413	▨	⌐	●
3326	▨		959	—		310	■	⌐	●

DMC Floss

	X st		X st		X st		X st	BS
743		666		718		958		
741		209		996		703		
947		208		322		310		
893								

DMC Floss

	X st	BS		X st	BS		X st	BS
White	⊡		598			415		
776			806		⌐ 414			
957			402			317		
309		⌐ 922			3799		⌐
209			762					

47

Home Sweet Home

Bottom Left

Bottom Right

DMC Floss

	X st	BS	FK		X st	BS	FK		X st	BS	FK		X st	BS	FK	LS
White	⊡			3713	☐			3761	◉			927	☐				
745	☐			3716	☐			3766	☐	⌐		402	☐				
676	☐			3733	⊞	⌐		369	☐			977	N	⌐			
741	☐			3731	♥	⌐	●	368	⊡	⌐		437	☐				
945	☐			340	☐	⌐		320	☐	⌐	●	3827	⊠				
758	⊟			3753	☐			504	✳			413	■	⌐	●		
351	☐			813	☐	⌐	●	928	△			310	⊡	⌐	●	/
349	■	⌐	●	747	☐												

DMC Floss

	X st	BS		X st	BS	FK
White	·		472			
676			907	+		
351			989			
350	▣		986	■	⌐	
349			739	⊠		
817		⌐	738			
899			437	N		
321	▣		435			
211			434	⊡		
209			433		⌐	
369			402			
368	−		301	◉		
367			3799	■	⌐	●
772	⊠					

DMC Floss		
	X st	BS
White	⊡	
712	⬜	
743	⊡	
760	⊟	
3326	⬜	
899	▽	
326	⬛	⌐
3753	⊠	
3755	⬜	⌐
799	⊙	
930		⌐⌐
312	⬛	⌐
3348	⬜	
988	⬜	
955	◩	
954	⬜	
911	⬛	⌐
543	⁂	
739	⬜	
437	N	
435	⬜	⌐
433	E	
841	⬜	
898	⬛	⌐
762	⬜	
318	⬜	
317	◇	
413	⬛	⌐

DMC Floss								
	X st	BS		X st	BS		X st	BS
676			813			319		
223			825			420		
3721			320			310		

Plenty and Grace be to this Place

DMC Floss

X st

676	
223	
3721	
813	
825	
320	
319	
420	
647	
535	
310	

DMC Floss

	X st	BS	FK
746	□		
745	H		
676			
353	–		
818	△		
776			
899			
321	▣		
498	★		
815		⌐	
223			
3721		⌐	●
211			
209			
747			
3766	◎		
807			
800	+		
809			
813			
825	▣		
320			
319		⌐	
420			
647			
535		⌐	
414		⌐	
3799	❄	⌐	
310	■		●

DMC Floss

	X st	BS
White	·	⌐
745		
743	△	
742		
554		
553		
552	⊡	
550	■	
3325		
799	★	
747		
3766	○	
807		⌐
3363		
3053	⊡	
3052		
3051		
563		
561		
400		
413		⌐

DMC Floss					
	X st	BS		X st	BS
White	·	⌐	813	◼	
744	◎		825	◼	⌐
742	◼		3364	◼	
741	◼		3363	◼	
740	◼		368	◼	
818	◻		367	▽	
776	⊡		504	◼	
3713	+		502	◼	
760	◼		501		⌐
3328	◼		3776	+	
347		⌐	400	◼	
3747	◻		918		⌐
341	◼		762	◼	
340	◼		414		⌐
333		⌐	413		⌐
827	N				

DMC Floss

	X st	BS		X st	BS
White	⊡		954	▨	
745	✳		911	■	
743	⊡		402	▨	⌐
970	▨		3776	+	
760	☐	⌐	762	▨	
3731	▨	⌐	318	▨	
606	▣	⌐	317	◈	
210	▨	⌐	413	■	⌐
367	◉	⌐			

DMC Floss			
	X st	BS	FK
White	⊡		
712	▢		
745	✳		
3708	▬		
3779	▢		
3778	▨		
606	⊡		
817	▨	⌐	
321	★	⌐	
211	✛		
209	▨		
3609	▢		
327		⌐	
800	▨		
334	▨		
312	▨	⌐	
563	▨		
562	▨		
561		⌐	
988	▨		
986	■		
469	K	⌐	
437	▢		
435	▨		
433	▨		
400	◇	⌐	
898		⌐	
762	▢		
317		⌐	
413			
310	■	⌐	●

DMC Floss

	X st	BS		X st	BS
White	·		826	▨	⌐
744	△		825	▨	
743	✚	⌐	798	▣	
742	▨		564	⊠	
970	▨		563	▨	
606	✚		3348	▨	
817	▪	⌐	988	▨	
3609	▨		469	▨	
340	★		986	▪	⌐
333	▪		739	▨	
828	▨		436	▨	
827	▨		433	▪	⌐
775	▨		414		⌐
813	✚		317		⌐

66

DMC Floss			
	X st	**BS**	**LD**
743			
676			
782			
351			
349			
3726			
223			
3721			
3609			
800			
322			
312			
931			
930			
369			
320			
3809			
3348			
3347			
3345			
739			
433			
801			
414			
310			

DMC Floss

	X st	BS
White	⊡	
676		
818		
776	◎	
3731		⌐
3726		
210		⌐
340	★	
798	▣	⌐
931		
930	+	
597	△	
564	⊠	
320		
367		⌐
3809	★	
839		
414		⌐

Kindred Spirits

Dentist
Husband
Sister
Brother
Father
Mother

If friends were flowers I'd pick you.

NOPQRSTUVWXYZ
stuvwxyz-1234567890

Bottom Right

Code for Pages 72-75

DMC Floss	X st	BS	FK	LS	LD
White	⊡				
746	☐				
744	☐				
742	⊞	⌐			
740	▦	⌐			
754	☐				
776	☐				
899	▦	⌐			
309	■	⌐	●		
498	★	⌐			
210	▦	⌐			
208	■	⌐	●		
775	☐				
3752	△				
3755	⊡	⌐			
312	■	⌐			
471	▦	⌐			⬭
564	G				
320	▦	⌐	●		⬭
561	■	⌐	●		
738	⊙				
436	N				
434	▦				
300	■	⌐			
648	▦				
646	▦	⌐	●	/	
310	⊡	⌐	●	/	

Code for Pages 76-77

DMC Floss

	X st		X st	BS	FK
White	·	797		⌐	●
745		747			
727	⊡	959			
725		3765			
3712	+	955	○		
349		502			
3609		436			
3607		976			
931		415			
930	⊡	3799	△	⌐	
799	−	310	■	⌐	●
798					

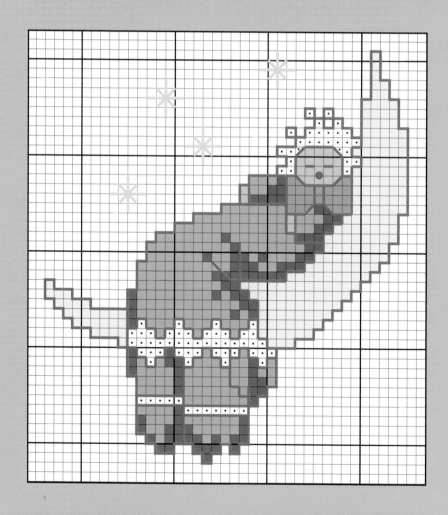

DMC Floss			
	X st	BS	FK
White	·		
746			
744			
743			
951			
776			
3609			
350			
800			
334	·		
312			
964			
958			
435			
839			
646			●
3799			
310	■		●

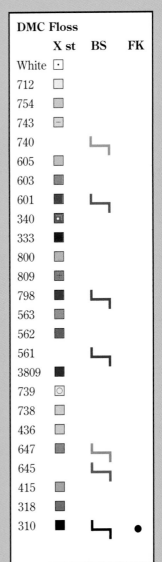

DMC Floss

	X st	BS	FK
White	⊡		
712			
754			
743	−		
740		⌐	
605			
603			
601		⌐	
340			
333			
800			
809			
798		⌐	
563			
562			
561		⌐	
3809			
739	◎		
738			
436			
647		⌐	
645		⌐	
415			
318			
310		⌐	●

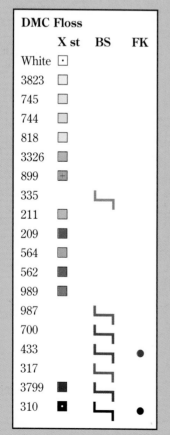

DMC Floss

	X st	BS	FK
White	⊡		
3823			
745			
744			
818			
3326			
899			
335		⌐	
211			
209			
564			
562			
989			
987		⌐	
700		⌐	
433		⌐	●
317		⌐	
3799	■	⌐	
310	■	⌐	●

DMC Floss

	X st		X st	BS		X st	BS		X st	BS		X st	BS		X st	BS
White	⊡	606	■	⌐	210	△		3325	◉	3765	■	⌐	839	■		
745	□	892	■		209	■		826	■	563	■		317			⌐
3341	⊡	350	▣		208	■	⌐	747	□	402	⊠	⌐	3799	■		⌐
3340	▨	211	□		775	▯		598	⊞	433	■					

DMC Floss

	X st		X st		X st		X st	BS		X st		X st		X st	BS		X st	BS
White	⊡	3326		3766		312			738	921		841			762			
3045		666		322		989			402	842		938			310			

DMC Floss

	X st	BS		X st	BS	FK
White	·		3761	+		
745			797		⌐	
740		⌐	3765		⌐	
3689	◎		772			
3688			988		⌐	
3687		⌐	435			
3607		⌐	413	■	⌐	●
349	■	⌐				

DMC Floss

	X st	BS		X st	BS
White	⊡		813	▨	
744	▢		826	N	
945	▢		824		⌐
402	⊞		964	▣	
776	▢		959	▨	
899	▨		966	▢	
211	▢		563	⊡	
210	◎		319		⌐
209	▨		610	▨	
208		⌐	801	■	⌐
3753	⊡		413		⌐
827	▢				

A Mother's Love

Knows no End

DMC Floss

	X st	BS
White	·	
744		
945		
353	+	
776		
899		⌐
3609	◎	
800		⌐
322		
966	·◌	⌐
959		
402		
415		
413	■	⌐
310	■	└

DMC Floss		
	X st	BS
743	▪	
5282		
957	▪	
800	▪	
312		
400		

Love & Friendship

Bottom Left

Bottom Right

Code for Pages 90-93

DMC Floss

	X st	BS	FK
White	⊡		
3823	☐		
677	⊙		
676	☐		
729	☐		
225	☐		
224	☐		
223	☐	⌐	
3722	☐		
3721		⌐	●
211	☐		
340	☐		
3746		⌐	●
3325	☐		
3755	⊞		
322	☐	⌐	
312	☐	⌐	●
524	☐		
3364	☐		
3362		⌐	
945	☐		
402	☐		
3827	△		
434		⌐	●
433		⌐	●
318	☐		
317		⌐	●
3799	■	⌐	●

Code for Pages 94-95

DMC Floss

	X st	BS
745	☐	
744	☐	
743	⊙	
742	☐	
727	✳	
726	⊞	
761	☐	
760	⊞	
3350	■	
554	☐	
552	■	
340	☐	
333	■	
320	⊙	
502	☐	
501	☐	
911	☒	
434		⌐

Code for Page 96

DMC Floss			
	X st	**BS**	**Bds**
White	⊡		
745	▦		
743	▣		
676	⊞		
948	▦		
754	▦		
758	▬		
3326	▦		
3607	■		
3756	▦		
800	▦		
3755	⊡		
322	▦		
312	■	⌐	
3347	▦		
3346	◉		
3345	▦	⌐	
301	▦	⌐	
317	▦	⌐	
White			⊠
Silver			▦

DMC Floss

	X st	BS	FK
White	⊡		
3823	☐		
745	−		
743	☐		
741	▨	⌐	
754	☐		
225	☐		
224	▨	⌐	
223	▨		
3722	▨	⌐	
3761	☐		
519	▨		
518	▨	⌐	
3760	▨	⌐	
517	■	⌐	●
3816	⊡		
3815	▨		
500		⌐	
435	▨		
839	■		
310		⌐	●

DMC Floss

	X st	BS		X st	BS
White	·		825	■	
743	◎		993	■	
818	−		3814	■	
3354	■	⌐	988	■	
3722	■	⌐	986	■	⌐
3712	+		3773	■	
347	■		738	■	
816	◻		436	■	
554	■		762	■	
552	■	⌐	318	■	
3753	■		413	■	
827	■		310	■	⌐

DMC Floss

	X st	BS		X st		X st	BS
White	·		3756	☐	3346	☐	
745	☐		3761	–	319	–	⌐
744	☐		800	△	402	☐	⌐
743	+		809	◼	801		
353	☐		966	☐	415		⌐
350		⌐	563	·	317	◼	
3326	·		3348	☐	413	◼	⌐
211	☐						

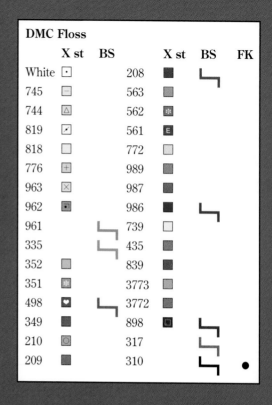

DMC Floss

	X st	BS		X st	BS	FK
White	⊡		208	■	⌐	
745	⊟		563	■		
744	△		562	✳		
819	⊡		561	E		
818	▢		772	▢		
776	+		989	■		
963	⊠		987	■		
962	⊡		986	■	⌐	
961			739	▢		
335		⌐	435	■		
352	■		839	■		
351	✳		3773	■		
498	♥	⌐	3772	■		
349	■		898	⊡	⌐	
210	○		317	■	⌐	
209	■		310	■	⌐	●

DMC Floss

	X st	BS		X st
3823	☐		210	◉
745	⊟		209	◼
743	☐		208	◼
741	◻	⌐	3325	◻
676	◻		334	▨
3045	◼		955	◻
225	☐		912	Ⓗ
224	▨		910	◼
223	◼		3813	△
776	⊞		3816	▨
899	◼		3815	◼
309	◼	⌐	500	
211	☐		317	

DMC Floss		
	X st	**BS**
White	⊡	
3823	△	
744	▦	
729	▦	
963	⊞	
3716	▦	
962	⊡	
961	▦	⌐
666	▦	
498		⌐
775	▦	
800	⊙	
3761	▦	
518	▦	
3760	⊞	
517	▦	
739	▦	
842	▦	
840	▦	
839	▦	
950	▦	
3772	▦	
632		⌐
453	▦	
452	▦	
535		⌐
310	▪	⌐

DMC Floss

	X st	BS		X st	BS
White	·		796	■	
745	ı		989	▦	
744	▦		987	▦	
948	▦		563	▦	
754	▦	⌐	562	⊡	
353	⊙		561	▦	
818	−		976	▦	
3326	▦		762	▦	
899	+	⌐	414	▦	
3756	▦		317	▦	⌐
799	▦		310	■	⌐

DMC Floss

	X st	BS	FK
White			
3823			
744			
722			
720			
818			
776			
3326			
309			
3688			
3803			
931			
3064			
632			
801			
3024			
648			
647			
415			
451			
535			
310			

DMC Floss

	X st	BS		X st	BS
White	·		792	■	⌐
3823	☐		368	▨	
745	✳		367	▨	
727	☐		911	✕	
3045		⌐	3364	▨	
818	—		3363	⊡	
3326	▨		3779	—	
3733	⊿		3778	⊙	
3350	■		317		⌐
211	▨		413		⌐
209	▨	⌐			

DMC Floss

	X st		X st	BS
White	·	825	▨	▨
743	▨	809	▨	
349	▨	469	▨	⌐
827	▨			

Mother Nature

Little deeds
of kindness
Little words

of love
Make our Earth
an Eden
like the heavens
above

Bottom Left

112

ONE IS NEARER TO GOD IN THE GARDEN

Code for Pages 110-113

DMC Floss

X st	BS	FK	LS	X st	BS	FK	LS	X st	BS	FK	LS
White				327	⌐		\	3816			
745				3753				561	⌐	●	
743				809				739	⌐		
742	⌐			793	⌐			402			\
676				964				3776	⌐		
951				992				3827			
945				598				977			
352				597	⌐			301	⌐		
350		●		369				3773			
776				966				3772			
3733				989				801	⌐	●	\
3731				987	⌐	●		762			
3350	⌐	●	\	955				318			
3608				913				317	⌐	●	
209				3817				310	⌐	●	

Code for Pages 114-115

DMC Floss

	X st	BS	FK
White	·		
Ecru	▢		
745			
776			
899		⌐	
800			
799	✕		
798	■		
772			
3347			
3346	E		
895	◱	⌐	
320			
319	■	⌐	
3047			
372			
3828	◎		
370			
869			
433		⌐	●
839	■	⌐	
310	■	⌐	●

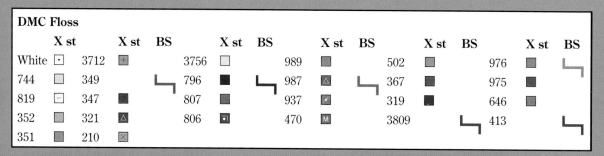

DMC Floss

X st		X st		BS		X st	BS		X st	BS		X st	BS		X st	BS		X st	BS
White	⊡	3712	⊞		3756	☐		989	■		502	■		976	■		
744	☐	349			796	■		987	△		367	■		975	■		
819	⊟	347	■		807	■		937	⟋		319	■		646	■		
352	☐	321	△		806	⊡		470	M		3809			413			
351	■	210	⊠														

DMC Floss

	X st	BS		X st	BS		X st	BS
725	◇		930	■		3348	◻	
783	■		799	▽		987	◻	⌐
3609	◻		797	■		368	◻	
351	■	⌐	747	◻		367	■	
224	◻		959	▨		402	◻	
223	◻		597	■		3776	■	
221	■	⌐	806	■		301	■	⌐
3753	▨		3810	■		801	■	
932	◻		772	◻		414	■	⌐
931	⊞							

DMC Floss

	X st	BS		X st	BS		X st
White	⊡		778			501	⊠
783		⌐	316			368	
352			315			320	⌐
350			932			367	
817	⊙	⌐	931	⊡		319	
899	⊡		930		⌐	839	
309		⌐	502				

DMC Floss

	X st	BS
3827		
3326		
335		
326		
554		
552		⌐
550		
3348		
3345		⌐
988		
986		
433		

DMC Floss

	X st		X st		X st	BS	FK
White	⊡	210		825			
743		208		798	+		
741		550		975			
783		3685		938	✳		
722		3761		3799			
349		813	★	310	▪		●
900							●

DMC Floss

	X st	BS	FK
White			
3823			
744			
742			
3827			
3340			
350			
3817			
3816			
976			
434			
433			
840			
317			
310			

DMC Floss

	X st		X st		X st	BS	FK
White	⊡	326	N	798	⊞		
744	☐	208	■	703	▨		
743	⊡	3685	■	646	▨		●
741	▨	747	☐	938	✳		●
783	◎	3766	▨	3799	▨		●
722	▨	3760	△	413	■		
720	▨	813	★	310	■		
900	☐	825	▨				

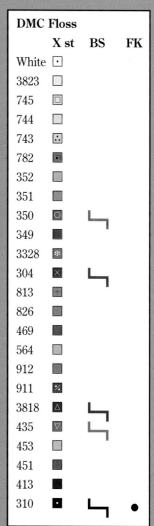

DMC Floss

	X st	BS	FK
White	⊡		
3823	▢		
745	▣		
744	▨		
743	⊡		
782	⊡		
352	▨		
351	▨		
350	⊙	⌐	
349	◼		
3328	❋		
304	⊠	⌐	
813	⊞		
826	▨		
469	▨		
564	▨		
912	▨		
911	◪		
3818	◭	⌐	
435	▽	⌐	
453	▨		
451	▨		
413	◼		
310	◼	⌐	●